WILMER VALDERRAMA

LOVE, LEGACY, AND ADVOCACY IN THE WORLD OF ENTERTAINMENT

Exceptional Exploration of American Famous Actor True Life Events, Career Achievements, and Impact in the Hollywood Industry

SOPHIA HARTCROWN

COPYRIGHT © 2024 SOPHIA HARTCROWN

All rights reserved. No part of this publication may be reproduced, distributed, or transmitted in any form or by any means, including photocopying, recording, or other electronic or mechanical methods, without the prior written permission of the publisher, except in the case of brief quotations embodied in critical reviews and certain other noncommercial uses permitted by copyright law.

TABLE OF CONTENTS

INTRODUCTION

CHAPTER 1: Early Life and Career Beginnings

Birth and Background

Introduction to Acting

Debut Roles and Breakthrough with "That '70s Show"

CHAPTER 2: Television and Film Career

Notable Roles on Screen

Voice Acting and Animation Work

Expansion into Film and Production Ventures

CHAPTER 3: Philanthropy and Activism

Global Ambassadorship for USO

Advocacy Work with Voto Latino

Co-founding Harness and Social Impact

CHAPTER 4: Musical Pursuits

Musical Alter Ego: Eduardo Fresco

Collaborations and Music Releases

Crossing Over: Spanish and English Tracks

CHAPTER 5: Personal Life and Relationships

Romances with Mandy Moore, Lindsay Lohan, and Demi Lovato

Engagement to Amanda Pacheco and Fatherhood

Passion for Cars and Collecting

CHAPTER 6: Legacy and Impact

Cultural Influence and Representation

Contributions to the Entertainment Industry

Future Endeavors and Continuing Influence

CONCLUSION

INTRODUCTION

In the vibrant tapestry of American entertainment, few figures shine as brightly and diversely as Wilmer Eduardo Valderrama. Born on January 30, 1980, Valderrama's journey from Miami, Florida, to the heights of Hollywood stardom is a testament to talent, perseverance, and a relentless commitment to making a difference.

This book delves deep into the life and career of Wilmer Eduardo Valderrama, tracing his trajectory from humble beginnings to becoming a multifaceted actor, activist, and cultural icon. From his early years spent in Venezuela to his eventual return to the United States, Valderrama's upbringing laid the foundation for a career that would transcend borders and boundaries.

Chapter 1 explores the formative experiences of Valderrama's childhood and his introduction to the world of acting. From his first forays into theater productions to landing his breakout role as Fez in the beloved sitcom "That '70s Show," this chapter unveils the early milestones that shaped his career.

In Chapter 2, readers are taken on a journey through Valderrama's extensive work in television and film. From his memorable portrayal of quirky characters to his ventures into animation and voice acting, Valderrama's versatility as an actor shines through. This chapter also highlights his forays into film production and his role as a cultural ambassador on the small and silver screens.

Valderrama's commitment to making a difference extends beyond the realm of entertainment, as detailed in Chapter 3. Through his involvement with organizations like the United Service Organizations (USO) and Voto Latino, he leverages his platform to advocate for social causes close to his heart. Co-founding the non-profit organization Harness underscores his dedication to effecting meaningful change in the world.

Chapter 4 delves into Valderrama's lesser-known yet equally impactful pursuit: music. Under the guise of his alter ego, Eduardo Fresco, he explores his passion for music, collaborating with artists across genres and languages. This chapter offers insight into his creative process and his vision for bridging cultural divides through music.

Despite the glitz and glamour of Hollywood, Valderrama's personal life is not immune to scrutiny. Chapter 5 delves into his high-profile romances with fellow celebrities and his journey to finding love and starting a family. Additionally, readers gain insight into his other passion: collecting cars and preserving cultural artifacts from his iconic role on "That '70s Show."

Finally, Chapter 6 reflects on the enduring legacy of Wilmer Eduardo Valderrama. Through his contributions to entertainment and activism, he leaves an indelible mark on popular culture and paves the way for future generations of

Latinx talent. As readers reflect on his journey, they are inspired by his resilience, creativity, and unwavering commitment to making the world a better place.

In celebrating the life and career of Wilmer Eduardo Valderrama, this book aims to honor his accomplishments, shed light on his impact, and inspire readers to pursue their own dreams with passion and purpose.

CHAPTER 1

Early Life and Career Beginnings

In this chapter, we delve into the formative years of Wilmer Eduardo Valderrama's life and the beginnings of his remarkable career in the entertainment industry. From his birth in Miami, Florida, to his upbringing in Venezuela, we explore the cultural influences and experiences that shaped his identity and aspirations. Discover how a young Valderrama found his passion for acting, from early performances in school plays to his professional debut in commercials and television miniseries. Follow his journey as he navigates the challenges and opportunities of pursuing a career in Hollywood, culminating in his breakout role as Fez in the iconic sitcom "That '70s Show." Through anecdotes and insights, we uncover the defining moments and decisions that set the stage for Valderrama's enduring legacy in the world of entertainment.

Birth and Background

Wilmer Eduardo Valderrama entered the world on January 30, 1980, in the vibrant city of Miami, Florida. Born to Balbino A. and Sobeida Valderrama, Wilmer's roots reflect a rich tapestry of cultural heritage. His father hails from Venezuela, while his mother is Colombian, imbuing him with a diverse blend of Latin American influences from an early age.

At the tender age of three, Wilmer's family embarked on a journey that would shape his formative years profoundly. They made the pivotal decision to relocate to Venezuela, where Wilmer would spend the next decade of his life immersed in the vibrant culture of his father's homeland. It was in Venezuela that Wilmer's passion for storytelling and performance began to take root, nurtured by the colorful tapestry of Latin American music, art, and folklore that surrounded him.

Despite the warmth and familiarity of Venezuela, Wilmer's family eventually made the bittersweet decision to return to the United States when he was thirteen years old. Settling back in the U.S., Wilmer faced the challenges of adjusting to a new environment while grappling with the complexities of his multicultural identity. However, it was this blend of experiences that would ultimately become a source of strength and inspiration in his artistic journey.

Introduction to Acting

Wilmer Valderrama's journey into the world of acting began with a serendipitous encounter that would change the course of his life forever. Encouraged by a drama teacher who recognized his natural talent and charisma, Wilmer took his first tentative steps onto the stage, embracing the transformative power of performance with open arms.

Fuelled by a passion for storytelling and a desire to connect with others on a deeper level, Wilmer embarked on a journey of self-discovery through the art of acting. He honed his craft through participation in numerous school plays and community theater productions, eagerly soaking up knowledge and experience with each new opportunity.

But it was a fateful encounter with a talent agent that would propel Wilmer into the spotlight and set him on the path to stardom. Recognizing his raw talent and magnetic presence, the agent saw potential in Wilmer and wasted no time in securing his auditions for television and film roles.

Debut Roles and Breakthrough with "That '70s Show"

Wilmer Valderrama's ascent to stardom reached new heights with his breakthrough role as Fez in the hit television sitcom "That '70s Show." Cast as the lovable foreign exchange student with a penchant for mischief and charm, Wilmer captivated audiences with his infectious energy and comedic timing.

From the moment he graced the screen, Wilmer's portrayal of Fez resonated with viewers, earning him widespread acclaim and adoration. His endearing quirks and misadventures endeared him to fans worldwide, solidifying his status as a rising star in Hollywood.

As "That '70s Show" became a cultural phenomenon, Wilmer's star continued to rise, affording him a platform to showcase his talents and expand his horizons. With each passing season, he evolved as an actor, exploring new facets of his character and leaving an indelible mark on the hearts of audiences everywhere.

But beyond the laughter and applause, Wilmer's success on "That '70s Show" represented more than just a career milestone – it was a testament to his perseverance, passion, and unwavering dedication to his craft. With Fez, Wilmer had found his muse, breathing life into a character that would forever be etched in the annals of television history.

CHAPTER 2

Television and Film Career

In this chapter, we delve into Wilmer Eduardo Valderrama's expansive journey through the realms of television and film. From his humble beginnings as a budding actor to his emergence as a multifaceted talent on both the small and silver screens, Wilmer's career trajectory is a testament to his versatility, dedication, and boundless creativity.

Join us as we explore the diverse roles and projects that have defined Wilmer's television and film career. From iconic sitcoms to acclaimed dramas, Wilmer's ability to inhabit a wide range of characters has captivated audiences and earned him acclaim from critics and fans alike. Through insightful anecdotes and behind-the-scenes revelations, we uncover the moments that have shaped Wilmer's evolution as an actor and propelled him to the forefront of the entertainment industry.

Discover how Wilmer's passion for storytelling extends beyond acting, as he explores the world of animation and lends his voice to beloved characters on screen. From charming preschoolers as Manny in "Handy Manny" to embodying the heroic spirit of Prince Philippe Charming in "Charming," Wilmer's voice-acting prowess knows no bounds.

But Wilmer's contributions to entertainment extend far beyond his performances in front of the camera. As a producer and entrepreneur, he has played an instrumental role in bringing compelling stories to life and championing diverse voices in the industry. From founding his own production company to spearheading projects that challenge the status quo, Wilmer's impact on the landscape of television and film is undeniable.

Through triumphs and challenges, successes and setbacks, Wilmer's television and film career has been a testament to his resilience, passion, and unwavering commitment to his craft. Join us as we celebrate the highlights, explore the nuances, and uncover the hidden gems of Wilmer Eduardo Valderrama's extraordinary journey through the world of entertainment.

Notable Roles on Screen

Throughout his illustrious career, Wilmer Eduardo Valderrama has graced the screen with a diverse array of memorable roles, showcasing his remarkable range and versatility as an actor. From his breakout performance as Fez in "That '70s Show" to his portrayal of complex characters in acclaimed dramas, Wilmer's on-screen presence has captivated audiences and garnered critical acclaim.

One of Wilmer's most iconic roles is undoubtedly that of Fez, the lovable foreign exchange student with a penchant for mischief and charm, in the hit sitcom "That '70s Show." As Fez, Wilmer brought an infectious energy and comedic flair to the screen, endearing himself to fans worldwide and solidifying his status as a rising star in Hollywood. His portrayal of Fez remains etched in the annals of television history, earning him widespread acclaim and adoration.

Beyond "That '70s Show," Wilmer has proven himself to be a versatile actor capable of tackling a wide range of roles. In the medical drama "Grey's Anatomy," he portrayed Kyle Diaz, a patient undergoing treatment for multiple sclerosis, delivering a nuanced and poignant performance that resonated with audiences. His guest-starring role in the Netflix comedy series "The Ranch" further showcased his comedic chops, earning praise for his comedic timing and delivery.

Wilmer's commitment to portraying diverse characters extends beyond the realm of television, as evidenced by his work in acclaimed films such as "Lies & Illusions" and "The Adderall Diaries." In these roles, Wilmer has demonstrated his ability to inhabit complex characters with depth and authenticity, earning him recognition as a formidable talent in the world of film.

Voice Acting and Animation Work

In addition to his on-screen performances, Wilmer has made a significant impact in the world of animation and voice acting, lending his distinctive voice to a variety of beloved characters. One of his most notable voice roles is that of Manny Garcia in the Disney Channel animated series "Handy Manny." As the titular character, Wilmer brought warmth, charm, and humor to the role, making Manny a beloved figure among young audiences.

Wilmer's voice acting talents extend beyond children's programming, as evidenced by his portrayal of Rodrigo in the animated film "Clifford's Big Movie." In this role, Wilmer imbued the character with personality and charm, bringing him to life in a way that resonated with audiences of all ages.

In addition to his work in animation, Wilmer has lent his voice to various video games, including the popular "Scarface: The World Is Yours." In the game, he voiced the character of Manny Ribera, bringing depth and authenticity to the role.

Wilmer's contributions to the world of animation and voice acting have earned him widespread praise and recognition, solidifying his status as a versatile talent capable of bringing characters to life in captivating and memorable ways.

Expansion into Film and Production Ventures

As Wilmer's career has continued to evolve, he has expanded his horizons beyond acting to pursue ventures in film production and entrepreneurship. In 2003, he made his feature film debut in "Party Monster," a crime drama based on the true story of the notorious club promoter Michael Alig. In the film, Wilmer portrayed DJ Keoki, earning praise for his portrayal of the enigmatic character.

Since then, Wilmer has continued to explore opportunities in film, both in front of and behind the camera. In addition to his acting roles, he has ventured into film production, establishing his own production company, WV Entertainment. Through his production company, Wilmer has championed diverse voices and stories, seeking to create opportunities for underrepresented talent in the entertainment industry.

In 2015, Wilmer starred in "The Adderall Diaries," a psychological thriller based on the memoir of the same name by Stephen Elliott. In the film, he portrayed the character of Josh, a troubled young man caught up in a web of deceit and obsession. Wilmer's performance was praised by critics, who lauded his ability to convey the complexities of the character with depth and nuance.

In addition to his work in film production, Wilmer has also explored opportunities in other areas of entrepreneurship, including fashion and philanthropy. In 2007, he launched his own men's fashion label, "Calavena," showcasing his passion for style and design. He has also been actively involved in philanthropic efforts, serving as a Global Ambassador for the United Service Organizations (USO) and working with organizations such as Voto Latino to promote social change and empower communities.

Through his ventures in film production and entrepreneurship, Wilmer has demonstrated his commitment to using his platform to create positive change and uplift others. Whether on screen or behind the scenes, his passion for storytelling and dedication to making a difference continues to inspire audiences around the world.

CHAPTER 3

Philanthropy and Activism

In this chapter, we delve into Wilmer Eduardo Valderrama's profound commitment to philanthropy and activism, exploring how he utilizes his platform to effect positive change and advocate for causes close to his heart. From his role as a Global Ambassador for the United Service Organizations (USO) to his involvement with organizations like Voto Latino, Wilmer's dedication to making a difference extends far beyond the realms of entertainment.

Throughout his career, Wilmer has demonstrated a steadfast commitment to supporting and uplifting communities in need. As a Global Ambassador for the USO, he has traveled extensively to visit troops stationed around the world, bringing comfort, entertainment, and a touch of home to those serving their country. Through his interactions with service members and their families, Wilmer has gained a deep appreciation for their sacrifices and has made it his mission to show them unwavering support and gratitude.

In addition to his work with the USO, Wilmer is actively involved with Voto Latino, an organization dedicated to empowering and mobilizing Latinx voters. As a prominent advocate for voting rights and civic engagement, Wilmer has used his platform to raise awareness about the importance of participating in the democratic process and amplifying the voices of underrepresented communities. Through voter registration drives, educational initiatives, and advocacy campaigns, he is committed to ensuring that every voice is heard and every vote counts.

However, Wilmer's philanthropic efforts extend beyond his work with these organizations. In 2015, he co-founded Harness, a non-profit organization dedicated to advancing social justice through the power of storytelling and community engagement. Through Harness, Wilmer and his team work to amplify the voices of marginalized communities, create spaces for dialogue and collaboration, and drive meaningful change on issues ranging from racial justice to immigration reform.

Wilmer's dedication to philanthropy and activism is rooted in his own experiences growing up as a first-generation American with immigrant parents. He understands firsthand the challenges and barriers that many individuals and communities face, and he is deeply committed to using his platform to create opportunities for others and drive positive change in the world.

Through his tireless advocacy, Wilmer Eduardo Valderrama serves as a powerful example of how one individual can make a difference and inspire others to join in the fight for a more just and equitable society. In this chapter, we explore the impact of his philanthropic work and the legacy he is building as a champion for social justice and human rights.

Global Ambassadorship for USO

As a Global Ambassador for the United Service Organizations (USO), Wilmer Eduardo Valderrama has demonstrated an unwavering commitment to supporting and uplifting service members and their families around the world. Founded in 1941, the USO has a long history of providing entertainment, programs, and services to military personnel and their loved ones, and Wilmer's involvement with the organization has furthered its mission in profound ways.

Wilmer's journey with the USO began with his desire to give back to those who serve and sacrifice for their country. Inspired by his own family's military background and the stories of service members he met throughout his career, Wilmer saw an opportunity to use his platform to bring joy, comfort, and a touch of home to troops stationed far from their loved ones.

As a Global Ambassador, Wilmer has participated in numerous USO tours and events, traveling to military bases around the world to meet with service members, sign autographs, and perform for audiences. These tours have taken him to countries such as Afghanistan, Iraq, South Korea, and Germany, where he has had the opportunity to connect with troops from all branches of the military and express his gratitude for their service.

Beyond the entertainment value of his appearances, Wilmer's presence as a Global Ambassador has had a profound impact on morale and morale. His genuine warmth, enthusiasm, and appreciation for the sacrifices made by service members have helped to boost spirits and foster a sense of camaraderie among troops stationed far from home.

In addition to his work with the USO, Wilmer has also been involved in various initiatives aimed at supporting veterans and military families. He has participated in fundraising events, awareness campaigns, and advocacy efforts to address the unique challenges faced by those who serve in the armed forces and their loved ones.

Through his Global Ambassadorship for the USO, Wilmer Eduardo Valderrama has made a lasting impact on the lives of service members and their families around the world. His dedication to supporting the military community and his tireless efforts to bring joy and comfort to those who serve are a testament to his character and his commitment to making a difference in the world.

Advocacy Work with Voto Latino

Wilmer Eduardo Valderrama's advocacy work with Voto Latino represents a powerful commitment to empowering and mobilizing Latinx voters to make their voices heard in the democratic process. Founded in 2004, Voto Latino is a non-profit organization focused on engaging, educating, and empowering young Latinx voters to participate in civic life and create positive change in their communities.

As a prominent Latinx actor and activist, Wilmer recognized the importance of civic engagement and political participation within the Latinx community. He saw an opportunity to use his platform to raise awareness about the importance of voting rights, encourage voter registration and turnout, and amplify the voices of underrepresented communities in the political process.

Through his advocacy work with Voto Latino, Wilmer has participated in voter registration drives, educational initiatives, and advocacy campaigns aimed at increasing political participation among Latinx youth. He has used his platform to raise awareness about key issues impacting the Latinx community, including immigration reform, healthcare access, and economic opportunity.

Wilmer's involvement with Voto Latino has also extended to his participation in voter mobilization efforts during election cycles. He has encouraged Latinx voters to exercise their right to vote and make their voices heard on issues that matter to them, emphasizing the importance of civic engagement as a means of creating positive change in society.

In addition to his work with Voto Latino, Wilmer has also been involved in other initiatives aimed at promoting social justice and political empowerment within the Latinx community. He has used his platform to advocate for policies that advance equity and justice, and he has spoken out against discrimination and injustice in all its forms.

Through his advocacy work with Voto Latino, Wilmer Eduardo Valderrama has made a significant impact on the political landscape, empowering Latinx voters to become active participants in the democratic process and shaping the future of our nation.

Co-founding Harness and Social Impact

Wilmer Eduardo Valderrama's co-founding of Harness represents a bold and innovative approach to driving social change and advancing social justice through the power of storytelling and community engagement. Founded in 2016, Harness is a non-profit organization dedicated to amplifying the voices of underrepresented communities, fostering dialogue and collaboration, and driving meaningful change on issues ranging from racial justice to immigration reform.

Driven by his own experiences as a first-generation American with Venezuelan and Colombian heritage, Wilmer recognized the power of storytelling as a tool for social transformation. He saw an opportunity to use his platform to elevate the voices of those whose stories are often overlooked or marginalized and to create spaces for dialogue and collaboration that inspire action and drive positive change.

Through Harness, Wilmer and his co-founders have launched a variety of initiatives aimed at advancing social justice and promoting civic engagement. These initiatives include storytelling workshops, community forums, and advocacy campaigns designed to raise awareness about key issues impacting underrepresented communities and mobilize individuals to take action.

One of Harness's most notable initiatives is its partnership with artists, activists, and organizations to create impactful content that raises awareness about social justice issues and inspires audiences to become agents of change. Through powerful storytelling and creative expression, Harness harnesses the power of art to provoke thought, spark conversation, and mobilize communities to take action on issues that matter.

In addition to its storytelling initiatives, Harness also works to provide resources and support to grassroots organizations and activists working on the front lines of social justice. Through its grant programs, training workshops, and mentorship opportunities, Harness helps to build capacity and empower individuals and organizations to create lasting change in their communities.

Through his co-founding of Harness, Wilmer Eduardo Valderrama has demonstrated a deep commitment to social impact and a belief in the power of storytelling to drive positive change in the world. His vision for a more just and equitable society continues to inspire others to join in the fight for a better world, one story at a time.

CHAPTER 4

Musical Pursuits

This chapter delves into another facet of Wilmer Eduardo Valderrama's creative journey, his exploration of musical pursuits. From his alter ego Eduardo Fresco to his collaborations across genres and languages, Wilmer's foray into music showcases his passion for expression and connection through sound.

In this chapter, we uncover the rhythms, melodies, and stories that have shaped Wilmer's musical endeavors. From his early experiences with music to his aspirations as a recording artist, Wilmer's journey through the world of music offers insight into the intersection of artistry and identity.

Join us as we explore the evolution of Wilmer's musical career, from his debut single "The Way I Fiesta" to his collaborations with artists from both the English and Spanish music scenes. Through anecdotes, interviews, and behind-the-scenes glimpses, we gain a deeper understanding of Wilmer's creative process and his vision for bridging cultural divides through music.

Through triumphs and challenges, successes and setbacks, Wilmer's musical pursuits serve as a testament to his creativity, passion, and unwavering commitment to artistic expression. In this chapter, we celebrate the melodies and harmonies that resonate with audiences around the world, offering a glimpse into the soul of an artist who continues to push boundaries and defy expectations through the power of music.

Musical Alter Ego: Eduardo Fresco

Wilmer Eduardo Valderrama's exploration of music takes a unique turn with his alter ego, Eduardo Fresco. As a musician, Wilmer sought to embrace a different persona, one that allowed him to experiment with sound, style, and storytelling in new and unexpected ways.

Under the guise of Eduardo Fresco, Wilmer embarked on a creative journey that blurred the lines between reality and fantasy. With his alter ego, he found the freedom to explore different facets of his identity and express himself through music in a way that felt authentic and liberating.

Eduardo Fresco represented a departure from Wilmer's on-screen persona, allowing him to shed the constraints of typecasting and embrace a more multifaceted approach to his artistry. With Eduardo Fresco, Wilmer could push the boundaries of creativity, blending genres and influences to create a sound that was uniquely his own.

Through Eduardo Fresco, Wilmer released his debut single "The Way I Fiesta" in 2011, accompanied by a music video directed by Akiva Schaffer of The Lonely Island fame. The song served as a playful introduction to Eduardo Fresco's world, blending infectious rhythms with tongue-in-cheek lyrics that celebrated the joy of living in the moment.

But Eduardo Fresco was more than just a musical alter ego – he was a persona that allowed Wilmer to connect with audiences on a deeper level, exploring themes of identity, self-expression, and cultural heritage through his music. With each song and performance, Eduardo Fresco invited listeners to join him on a journey of exploration and discovery, inviting them to embrace their true selves and celebrate the richness of life.

Collaborations and Music Releases

Wilmer Eduardo Valderrama's musical journey is characterized by a spirit of collaboration and experimentation, as he explores different genres and styles alongside a diverse array of artists. From his early collaborations with fellow musicians to his solo releases as Eduardo Fresco, Wilmer's music reflects a commitment to pushing boundaries and exploring new horizons.

Throughout his career, Wilmer has collaborated with artists from both the English and Spanish music scenes, showcasing his versatility and adaptability as a musician. Whether collaborating with established stars or emerging talent, Wilmer brings his unique energy and charisma to each project, elevating the music with his distinctive voice and style.

One notable collaboration is Wilmer's appearance in the music video for Wisin & Yandel's song "Imagínate" in 2009. In the video, Wilmer showcases his dancing skills and charismatic presence, adding an extra layer of excitement and energy to the song.

In 2011, Wilmer produced and appeared in the music video for LMFAO's hit single "Sexy and I Know It," further solidifying his reputation as a versatile entertainer with a flair for performance. His involvement in the video underscored his willingness to experiment with different genres and styles, showcasing his ability to adapt to diverse musical environments.

Like Eduardo Fresco, Wilmer released several tracks that showcased his musical versatility and eclectic tastes. From the infectious party anthem "The Way I Fiesta" to the introspective ballad "Salud Part 2," Eduardo Fresco's music offered a glimpse into Wilmer's creative vision and his desire to connect with audiences through the power of song.

Crossing Over: Spanish and English Tracks

Wilmer Eduardo Valderrama's musical journey transcends linguistic and cultural boundaries, as he explores the intersection of Spanish and English tracks in his repertoire. With a background that spans both Latin American and American influences, Wilmer embraces the richness of both languages, weaving together lyrics and melodies that speak to audiences across the globe.

One of Wilmer's earliest forays into Spanish-language music is his collaboration with the house music group Nomads on the song "Addicted to Love" in 2012. In the music video, Wilmer showcases his singing and dancing abilities, infusing the song with his trademark energy and charisma.

In addition to his collaborations with Spanish-speaking artists, Wilmer has also released English-language tracks that showcase his diverse musical influences and eclectic tastes. From the upbeat pop-rock vibes of "The Way I Fiesta" to the soulful balladry of "Salud Part 2," Wilmer's English-language music reflects a range of influences and styles, inviting listeners to join him on a journey of exploration and discovery.

But perhaps the most powerful aspect of Wilmer's music is its ability to bridge linguistic and cultural divides, bringing people together through the universal language of music. Whether singing in Spanish or English, Wilmer's music transcends language barriers, inviting listeners to connect with the emotions and experiences that unite us all.

Through his Spanish and English tracks, Wilmer Eduardo Valderrama demonstrates the power of music to transcend boundaries and bring people together. With each song and performance, he invites audiences to join him on a journey of exploration and discovery, celebrating the richness and diversity of the human experience through the universal language of music.

CHAPTER 5

Personal Life and Relationships

This chapter delves into the private world of Wilmer Eduardo Valderrama, offering a glimpse into the personal experiences and relationships that have shaped his life off-screen. From his early romances to his journey to fatherhood, Wilmer's personal life unfolds with its own unique blend of joys, challenges, and moments of reflection.

In this chapter, we explore the intricacies of Wilmer's relationships with loved ones, friends, and colleagues, shedding light on the human experiences that define his identity beyond the spotlight of Hollywood. From his high-profile romances with fellow celebrities to his deep-rooted connections with family and friends, Wilmer's personal life is a tapestry of love, laughter, and profound moments of growth.

Join us as we delve into the highs and lows of Wilmer's personal journey, from the excitement of new beginnings to the complexities of navigating fame and relationships in the public eye. Through intimate anecdotes and heartfelt reflections, we gain insight into the man behind the persona, uncovering the vulnerabilities and triumphs that make Wilmer Eduardo Valderrama a uniquely relatable figure in the realm of celebrity.

Through his personal experiences and relationships, Wilmer invites us to reflect on the universal themes of love, resilience, and self-discovery that resonate with us all. In this chapter, we celebrate the richness of Wilmer's personal life and the connections that remind us of our shared humanity amidst the glittering facade of stardom.

Romances with Mandy Moore, Lindsay Lohan, and Demi Lovato

Throughout his life, Wilmer Eduardo Valderrama has been romantically linked to several high-profile celebrities, including Mandy Moore, Lindsay Lohan, and Demi Lovato. These relationships have been the subject of much media scrutiny and speculation, offering glimpses into Wilmer's personal life and the complexities of love and celebrity in the public eye.

Wilmer's relationship with Mandy Moore dates back to the early 2000s when the two young stars crossed paths in Hollywood. Their romance captured the attention of fans and media alike, with rumors swirling about their budding relationship. Although they were both relatively young at the time, their connection seemed genuine, and they were often spotted together at events and premieres.

However, Wilmer's most high-profile relationship came in the mid-2000s when he began dating actress and pop star Lindsay Lohan. Their romance played out in the tabloids, with paparazzi capturing their every move and speculating about the nature of their relationship. Despite the media attention, Wilmer and Lindsay seemed to enjoy each other's company and were often seen out and about together in Los Angeles.

In 2010, Wilmer's romantic life once again made headlines when he began dating singer and actress Demi Lovato. Their relationship, which lasted on and off for six years, was marked by ups and downs, with both stars speaking openly about their struggles with addiction, mental health, and the pressures of fame. Despite the challenges they faced, Wilmer and Demi remained close friends and continued to support each other through their respective journeys to recovery.

While Wilmer's romantic relationships have often played out in the public eye, he has always maintained a level of privacy and discretion when it comes to his personal life. He has spoken candidly about the challenges of dating in Hollywood and the importance of finding genuine connections amidst the glare of the spotlight.

In the end, Wilmer's romances with Mandy Moore, Lindsay Lohan, and Demi Lovato offer a window into the complexities of love and relationships in the world of celebrity. Despite the ups and downs, the rumors and speculation, Wilmer has remained true to himself and his values, navigating the often tumultuous waters of romance with grace and integrity.

Engagement to Amanda Pacheco and Fatherhood

In January 2020, Wilmer Eduardo Valderrama announced his engagement to model Amanda Pacheco, marking a new chapter in his personal life and a cause for celebration among fans and friends alike. The couple's engagement came after nearly a year of dating, during which they had shared their love and adventures with followers on social media.

The announcement of their engagement was met with an outpouring of love and support from fans and friends, who were thrilled to see Wilmer find happiness and companionship with Amanda. The couple's love story captured the hearts of many, with their shared passion for travel, adventure, and each other shining through in every photo and post.

In December 2020, Wilmer and Amanda announced that they were expecting their first child together, adding another layer of joy and excitement to their relationship. The couple's journey to parenthood was documented on social media, with Wilmer sharing updates and photos of Amanda's pregnancy and their preparations for the arrival of their baby.

On February 15, 2021, Wilmer and Amanda welcomed their daughter into the world, marking a new chapter in their lives as parents. The couple's joy was evident as they shared photos and messages of love and gratitude with their followers, expressing their excitement and gratitude for the newest addition to their family.

As Wilmer embraces fatherhood, he does so with the same passion, dedication, and enthusiasm that he brings to every aspect of his life. He is committed to being a present and supportive father, offering love, guidance, and encouragement to his daughter as she grows and discovers the world around her.

For Wilmer, fatherhood is a profound and transformative experience, one that brings new meaning and purpose to his life. As he navigates the joys and challenges of parenthood, he does so with a sense of gratitude and humility, cherishing every moment and embracing the responsibility of shaping the future for his daughter.

Passion for Cars and Collecting

Beyond his work in entertainment and philanthropy, Wilmer Eduardo Valderrama has a deep passion for cars and collecting, which he has cultivated over the years into a diverse and impressive collection of vehicles. From vintage classics to modern supercars, Wilmer's love for automobiles is evident in the care and attention he devotes to his collection.

Wilmer's passion for cars dates back to his childhood when he developed an early fascination with automobiles and their design. As he grew older and found success in Hollywood, he began to indulge his passion for cars by acquiring and restoring classic vehicles, each one a testament to his love for automotive history and craftsmanship.

One of the crown jewels of Wilmer's collection is the original 1969 Oldsmobile Vista Cruiser used in "That '70s Show," which he purchased for $500 after learning that the show was going to cease production. The iconic car holds a special place in Wilmer's heart, serving as a cherished memento of his time on the beloved sitcom.

In addition to his vintage classics, Wilmer also owns a variety of modern supercars and luxury vehicles, which he enjoys driving and showcasing at car shows and events. His collection reflects his eclectic tastes and appreciation for automotive engineering, with each car representing a unique and cherished addition to his ever-growing fleet.

But for Wilmer, collecting cars is about more than just ownership – it's about preserving history, celebrating craftsmanship, and sharing his passion with others. He takes pride in his collection and enjoys sharing stories and insights about his cars with fellow enthusiasts, fostering a sense of community and camaraderie among fellow car lovers.

As Wilmer continues to expand his collection and explore new additions to his fleet, his passion for cars remains as strong as ever. Whether restoring a vintage classic or test-driving the latest supercar, Wilmer's love for automobiles is a lifelong passion that brings joy, excitement, and fulfillment to his life.

CHAPTER 6

Legacy and Impact

This chapter serves as a reflection on the enduring legacy and profound impact of Wilmer Eduardo Valderrama's life and career. It offers an exploration of the contributions he has made to the worlds of entertainment, philanthropy, and beyond, as well as the lasting impressions he has left on audiences and communities around the globe.

In this chapter, we delve into the multifaceted dimensions of Wilmer's legacy, examining how his artistic endeavors, philanthropic efforts, and personal journey have left an indelible mark on the cultural landscape. From his iconic roles on screen to his tireless advocacy for social justice,

Wilmer's impact transcends the boundaries of fame and celebrity, inspiring others to strive for positive change and meaningful engagement with the world around them.

Join us as we celebrate the moments of triumph, resilience, and transformation that define Wilmer's legacy. Through insightful reflections and poignant anecdotes, we honor the depth and breadth of his contributions to art, activism, and the human experience. In doing so, we recognize the enduring significance of Wilmer Eduardo Valderrama's life and work, and the profound impact he continues to have on generations to come.

Cultural Influence and Representation

Wilmer Eduardo Valderrama's cultural influence and representation in the entertainment industry are profound and far-reaching. As a first-generation American with Venezuelan and Colombian heritage, Wilmer embodies the rich diversity of the Latinx experience and serves as a powerful advocate for representation and inclusivity in Hollywood.

Throughout his career, Wilmer has used his platform to elevate stories and voices that reflect the complexities and nuances of the Latinx community. From his breakout role as Fez in "That '70s Show" to his advocacy work with organizations like Voto Latino, Wilmer has been a vocal proponent of greater diversity and representation in the media.

As a trailblazer in the entertainment industry, Wilmer has shattered stereotypes and defied expectations, challenging the notion of what it means to be a Latinx actor in Hollywood. Through his authentic portrayals of diverse characters and his commitment to telling stories that resonate with audiences of all backgrounds, Wilmer has paved the way for future generations of Latinx talent to thrive in the industry.

Wilmer's cultural influence extends beyond his on-screen work, as he uses his platform to champion social causes and advocate for positive change in the world. Whether through his philanthropic efforts or his involvement in initiatives that promote civic engagement and social justice, Wilmer continues to be a leading voice for progress and representation in the entertainment industry and beyond.

Contributions to the Entertainment Industry

Wilmer Eduardo Valderrama's contributions to the entertainment industry are vast and varied, spanning the realms of television, film, music, and beyond. From his breakout role as Fez in "That '70s Show" to his forays into music and philanthropy, Wilmer's impact on the industry is undeniable.

As Fez, Wilmer captured the hearts of audiences around the world with his endearing portrayal of the lovable foreign exchange student. His performance on the show not only solidified his status as a rising star in Hollywood but also paved the way for greater visibility and representation of Latinx actors on television.

In addition to his acting career, Wilmer has explored various other creative pursuits, including music and production. As Eduardo Fresco, he released several singles and music videos that showcased his musical talents and eclectic tastes. He also founded his own production company, WV Entertainment, through which he has championed diverse voices and stories in the industry.

Wilmer's impact on the entertainment industry extends beyond his artistic endeavors, as he uses his platform to advocate for social causes and promote positive change in the world. Through his work with organizations like the USO and Voto Latino, Wilmer continues to be a leading voice for progress and representation in the industry, inspiring others to use their platforms for good.

Future Endeavors and Continuing Influence

As Wilmer Eduardo Valderrama looks to the future, his influence on the entertainment industry shows no signs of waning. With a diverse array of projects in the works and a commitment to using his platform for positive change, Wilmer continues to be a driving force for progress and representation in Hollywood and beyond.

In the coming years, audiences can expect to see Wilmer continue to push boundaries and explore new creative avenues. Whether through his acting roles, musical endeavors, or philanthropic efforts, Wilmer remains dedicated to using his talents and platform to make a difference in the world.

As a trailblazer for diversity and representation in the entertainment industry, Wilmer's legacy will continue to inspire future generations of artists and activists to strive for greater inclusivity and equality. Through his continued influence and advocacy, Wilmer Eduardo Valderrama is helping to shape a more inclusive and equitable future for the world of entertainment and beyond.

CONCLUSION

In conclusion, the life and career of Wilmer Eduardo Valderrama are a testament to the power of perseverance, passion, and purpose. Through his journey from a young actor finding his footing in Hollywood to a multifaceted artist and advocate making a significant impact on and off the screen, Wilmer has left an indelible mark on the entertainment industry and beyond.

Throughout this book, we have explored the many facets of Wilmer's life and career, from his breakout role as Fez in "That '70s Show" to his forays into music, philanthropy, and activism. We have delved into the highs and lows of his personal journey, from the excitement of new beginnings to the challenges of navigating fame, relationships, and the complexities of identity in the public eye.

But beyond the glitz and glamour of Hollywood, Wilmer's story is one of resilience, authenticity, and unwavering commitment to his values. As a first-generation American with Venezuelan and Colombian heritage, Wilmer has used his platform to elevate stories and voices that reflect the richness and diversity of the Latinx experience. He has shattered stereotypes, challenged expectations, and championed representation and inclusivity in an industry often plagued by homogeneity.

Moreover, Wilmer's impact extends far beyond the realm of entertainment. Through his philanthropic efforts with organizations like the USO, Voto Latino, and Harness, Wilmer has worked tirelessly to make a positive difference in the world. He has used his voice to advocate for social justice, voting rights, and civic engagement, inspiring others to join him in the fight for a more equitable and inclusive society.

As we reflect on Wilmer's journey, one thing becomes abundantly clear: his legacy is one of inspiration, empowerment, and hope. He serves as a beacon of light for aspiring artists, activists, and changemakers everywhere, showing that with determination, authenticity, and a commitment to making a difference, anything is possible.

In the years to come, Wilmer's influence will continue to resonate, shaping the future of the entertainment industry and inspiring generations to come. As we bid farewell to this book, let us carry forward the lessons learned from Wilmer's journey – the importance of representation, the power of activism, and the enduring value of staying true to oneself – as we strive to create a better, more inclusive world for all.

Made in the USA
Monee, IL
01 May 2024